phases

phases

poems and musings
by
h.duxbury

Published by h.duxbury.

First printing, June 2020.

h.duxbury
Ontario, Canada

www.hduxburypoetry.com

ISBN: 978-1-7772131-0-7

For the ones who teach, read, love, listen to and share the stories that make up lives – you know who you are.

the phases

potential

we dream of roses

        and grow like

                weeds

Summer

the burn, the light, the passion

phases

creation

these stories squirm in me
insect larvae

caterpillars
that weave silk tents
and devour green leaves

I open my mouth
still hoping some beauty
will emerge from the cocoon of history
and fly from my lips

phases

cloud watching

where will we sit at the Apocalypse,
watching the end of the world
on the horizon?

you point at a cannonball
        a koala
        an angel
hiding in the clouds

4

seeing

the late afternoon sun

pierces

my eyes
a brilliant goddess
of life
and sight

vengeance
and blindness

she is here
and this day is almost at its end
my eyes weaken before the glory
soften and melt
pure sight

dripping

possibilities
into my brain

regret

I wish I could be sorry
that every kiss
was a crime
I didn't know we were committing

starving for beauty

let me dine
on the sweet nectar
condensing on your lips
as your inner warmth
meets the cool air
without

for we are all of us
starving
for beauty
and you are beautiful
as the fiercest storm

urban dreamscape

there are no stars
in this urban dreamscape
we howl at streetlight moons
and wish on the shooting stars
of passing headlights
we scream our names
under train bridges
and wait for an echo
to return them to us

celestials

I am not yours
you are not mine
we are two celestial bodies
orbiting
hearts floating in the stars
lips crashing like meteors
the pull of our gravity greater
than any ownership

fireflies

you were just like the fireflies
I never tried too hard to catch
always slipping through my hands
gone by midsummer

summer

wishless stars

we stood like giants
looking down
from highway overpasses
watching other worlds streak past
flaring and fading —
the after burn in our eyes
like shooting stars
that leave no wishes

headaches

there are still thunderstorms
behind my eyes
when I write about you

wordless

an idea hits
a wordless sense of enormity
stretching to infinity
within my skull
     and chest
in a moment of rushing words,
     unfelt sensations
     breathless amazement
I am more than human
     and less
and when it passes —
     why
there are no words at all

devotion

you are still
the first breath I want
to take each morning

connect the dots

I trace the freckles
on your shoulders
with my lips
connecting the dots
between your body
and your soul
between your soul
and mine

mangos

that summer
tastes
like mango

the fruit
and your name
sticky on my lips

both
deceptively sweet
hard at the centre

strawberry picnics

the flesh bursts
        shiny red surface parting
raining droplets like blood
        a sacrifice

your lips gleam red
        like desire
before your pink tongue swiftly
        erases the evidence

your blue eyes parody
        the early summer sky
taunting the nameless hue
        just above the horizon

we are so much more
        than the sum of parts
colours staining us
        bruises of identity

strawberries gleam red in
        the pristine white basket
sitting firmly on the earth
        between us

faith

you look at me
like for every wild
summer night's storm
you can still see the dawn's light
in my eyes

historic site histrionics

the sun is stark
      bright as all we can imagine
glittering and dancing on the river
turning the leaves above
into mirrors that reflect back at me,
below,
in a dark puddle of shade

this place is holy
it hums and sings
      of lovers with starry eyes
      quarrels and the rapport of fists
      childhood adventuring
      the wise musings of a lived life

it is familiar and distant
indifferent as the stones
that gleam on the shore

this is where I lost myself
to trees and waves
and fireflies in the dark places
and found myself
on dirty rocks
beside a murky river

linguistics

(After Caitlin Conlon)

in a language that doesn't have the word love, i say
'my feet are never warmer than when tangled with
yours'/i press my lips to yours like they are a
language i am desperate to be fluent in/ i say 'each
kiss is a treasure'/ i say 'i never noticed the stars this
way before you'/ i say 'suddenly a lifetime feels so
short'/ i reach my fingers toward yours in the dark/
and somehow yours always meet them

summer

at night

we melt into one another
our bodies pooling
in river valleys
of blankets and pillows
the warmth between us
greater
even than the heart
of the earth

the ones who stay

there are stories
like warm blankets
wrapped around us
made of
      long distance phone calls
      mix tapes
      and dreams whispered
      in bed at sleepovers

we've shared beds
for decades
growing through
      new bedrooms
      and young loves
from herbal tea and flannels
to wine and camisoles

as we learned
how some things just don't mix
      like milk in herbal tea
      or soft hearts in rough hands
and later
we learned how to put
      bed frames
      and hearts
back together
together

I don't know what magic
grows flowers of friendship
from phone lines
but
I will always have a bed
for you

pebbles

my father tells stories
of the first time
he flung himself into the sky
on manmade wings

of being told
to carry a pebble
on his tongue
to save his mouth
from fear

I have carried words
like pebbles
in my mouth
they roll around my tongue
hard nuggets of meaning
keeping me soft

there was a time
when the words ran dry
the fear hard
in my throat

I was throwing myself into the sky
praying my wings could hold
the weight of loss
I carried

the weight of freedom

I desperately pressed
my lips to yours
dreaming of softness
and finding
only a mouthful
of pebbles

hwy 17

we bake on the highway
an unforgiving sun burning
like judgement

I look upon bulrushes
pale bones long gone to seed
quietly rotting in the glare

ahead
smoke plumes in dark feathers
dispersing in a bad dream
above the glaring flames

the car is nestled against a pole
close as lovers in the chill of winter
this world has always demanded sacrifice

I look upon skeletons of bulrushes
rising from the side of the road
burning rubber seeping up my nose

arborists

there are those
for whom you could plant
entire forests
and they would still bemoan
the want
      of a single
            tree

phases

Autumn

the fade, the fall, the turning

phases

autumn

gold omens

golden leaves skitter
and swirl

unwanted invitations
to the dark season

bright harbingers
of a barren world

growing up

skipping over sidewalk cracks
so not to break my mother's back

I used to wonder what grown would be
someday the secrets would reveal to me

but here I am still stumbling
over sidewalk cracks
and my mother's back

passer-by

a stranger on the sidewalk
legs scissoring
arms swaying like rudders

they don't notice you
you don't notice them
alone together in this sidewalk world

but there's a question rattling chains
in the back of your mind

asking
who that person is
where they are going
and why —
will you see them again?

you turn your corner
lose sight of the stranger
you'll never know

dust

there is dust on my glasses

I have never been good
at clearing it

there is dirt under my nails
all the time it seems

I marvel
at the people
who do not keep some Earth
under their nails

who do not watch the world
through the fog
of life debris

flight

there is a white feather
tucked between the pages
of my notebook
I wonder who lost it
and
who clipped yours
so close
that you still bleed
when you try
to spread your wings —
even as I see flight
in your eyes

grey

I am every shade of grey
you ever met
the blurred book pages of late night binges
the exhausted asphalt under your boots
the heavy bruised shade of thunderclouds
when the air is dense with tension
always shifting
     crackling, crumpling
          moving on
          underfoot and overhead

autumn skies

this autumn sky is a bruise
swollen and blackblue
aching for resolution

anxiety

I've spent years
throwing myself off
the cliffs of my own mind

never certain
if I will land
on
        soft clouds
or
        jagged rocks

autumn

suppression

one day
you fear
they will find you
        dry-eyed
and
        water-logged

growing animosity

a school destroyed,
now a crumpled playground
for classless students,
the sun above baking dirt
into the corners and cracks
of a stolen opportunity

a child stoops
searching for treasure
in destruction

she doesn't know who did this
        but she knows their flag
and in her mind
        it will always fly
        over a ruined world.

stretch marks

I discovered
the first stretch mark
in a hotel bathroom
in grade eight

it curved over my left hip
delicate purple-blue
smooth like satin
softly shining

this soft blue line
filled me with terror
and something else—
the weight
and excitement
of impending adulthood
written in soft blue
on straining skin
about to leave childhood

sunrise from a bus window

Stiff vinyl seats, generic blue,
>   shining in the dim light
>   of a cold autumn morning.
The driver hits the brakes
>   unceremoniously —
>   jerking passengers
limp in unwelcome consciousness;
>   staring out dusty windows
>   with dull eyes
>   at shabby looking homes.
Sneaking glimpses
>   of a sunrise
>   more brilliant than their own
between worn walls and chimneys.
The bus jerks —
>   pulls up to the walk.
>   People rise and slowly depart,
>   their seats soon filled by others,
>   leaving no mark
>   on generic blue seats.

autumn

sunset thoughts

the sun is fading fast now
turning the sky
pastelcottoncandy colour
a squirrel leaps
a free silhouette
against peach and lemon
brilliantly indifferent
to my human woes

Orillia

I miss this town
sometimes--
the sunsets and silhouettes
the trails that kept my secrets
and the labyrinth of bus routes I'd take
that always guided me home safe
down roads with names
like poetry
      coldwater
      sundial
      memorial

but
it still looks like the barren white walls
of our home after the fall
there are
no happily ever afters in these
sidewalk cracks for me

letting go

this is the last poem
I will write for you
the last words I waste
on your lack of them

the last time I muse
on your gentle eyes
clever tongue
and deceptive heart

the last time I try
to dress up the truth
in pretty words
the way you dressed up lies

connections

we don't always have to see
eye to eye
when we are meeting
soul to soul

against the clock

ours
was a love against the clock
heartbeats dropping
like second hands

keeping our hearts
clutched to our chests
like pearls—
       beautiful and precious
       built in layers
       over the things that wound
we fell
holding ourselves aloft
holding each other aloft

telling ourselves
that the sands of time
would not be too heavy
to carry
that we were strong enough
to put this down
strong enough
to walk away

master of illusions

you spent years
planting red flags
convincing me
they were roses

directionally challenged

I am terrible at directions
my heart has too many poles
to lead me
the arrow always swinging round
to the places I have left pieces of myself
like soul litter
pointing to the bright hearts
whose gentle gravity
always pulls me back
always keeps my feet on the earth

time pieces

I turned around
and all that was left of us
were memories that
sift like sand
or salt
through
my fingers
when I try to
grasp anything
that could explain
how our friendship
could ever be reduced
to granules of fallen time
and a bitter taste

memory songs

drowning
in an old song
too much breath
rushing past my lips
I am filled with
early summer wind
pushing you away from me
like a ship
as my lungs collapse
into wet paper bags

apologies

I'm not sorry
for walking away
not sorry that your pretty lies
could not make me stay

autumn

The sidewalk is covered in leaves
      bright as gold
      shimmering with rain
      still ripe with the memory of life
they make
      quiet
            wet
                  noises
soft as flesh
      under my feet

This season always looks like death
but it
      like death
has always been about life

phases

Winter

the cold, the grief, the rest

phases

winter

in the winter forest

nothing moved
a world frozen
the space between heartbeats
the pause between breaths

an illusion of stillness
as pure as eternity
you cannot hear the tiny breaths below
or the heartbeats above

you can believe
that the ice is death
and the snow is a burden
when you are trapped in the cold above it

in the winter forest
all shades of grey
you can believe in magic
or you can forget it

frostbite

it was snowing that night
you had snowflakes on your eyelashes
your hand was cold,
        but I couldn't feel it
there was ice underfoot
and I was sliding
        but I didn't know it
stumbling on the words
frozen in my throat
I never knew what it was like
        to fall in love
but I fell into the snow
        and it melted down my back
I was freezing
        but I didn't notice it
as you helped me to my feet
        I only felt warm

loss

sometimes you find yourself
on the edge of something huge

an abyss in yourself you grew so comfortable with
that you forgot it existed

a yawning, vacant maw sitting between your heart
and your stomach

so you eat and you love and nothing fills the void.
and you strain and you reach and nothing closes it.
and you try to look into it. heaven knows you have
stared into the blackness and nothing shows through.

you know it is eating something.
you just can't remember what.

but sometimes you put your face so close that you can
almost smell it. that thing you lost.

remember?
that thing…

it's gone.

story of a home in a minor key

Did you hear that?
subtle hum,
rumbling bass growing closer,
great cello groans as something approaches
in the dark

Did you hear that?
a squeal,
high keening of old brakes and oboe
deep thud of bass drums and heavy work boots

Did you hear that?
glass breaking,
sharp notes hitting the ground
among the screech and cry of metal on wood
in violins and piccolo

Did you hear that?
smashing cymbals and crashing porcelain
the trickle of water barely heard on the triangle
steady snare of doors slammed open
staccato rhythm of running feet

...silence...

Can you hear this?

winter
low clarinet, deep parental groan of anguish
sharp peep of flute in a child's sob
light cymbal roll and a whispered

"our home..."

friendly ghost

sometimes
I still visit your ghost
I ask her
what she thinks of the world
now
I press my face against
death's door
and ask
are we still friends?
I say
I miss you

winter

arson

those days
when all of the words taste like ash
and burn in your throat
and every pen stroke
feels like a match scratching

when all of your meanings
smell like the smoke
of your scorched heart

If walls could see...
    they'd see smiles
    and tears.
    they would witness affairs,
    proposals,
    drug deals and dog fights;
    first dates and final goodbyes,
    marriages, births, divorces and deaths.

If walls could hear...
    they'd hear laughter and sobs;
    moans of pleasure,
    cries of joy,
    shrieks of fear,
    screams of pain
    and gasps of surprise.
    They'd hear secrets,
    plots and lies;
    promises
    and arguments.
    Nervous jokes and final blows;
    confessions
    and words of comfort.

If walls could speak...
    They would speak their minds—

winter

they would tell us of all
they have witnessed,
all they have known.

They would tell us of the frustration
of existing in silence —

they would never forget
the worth of a word.

the collector

I have kept
so many broken hearts
pressed
between the pages
of journals
and photo albums
all the frozen smiles
never betraying
the ugliness
       of our anger
or the colours we show
       when wounded

honesty

I used to believe truths
would beget truths
I spoke them like spells
to send lies
      skittering
into the night

spread them over my windowsills
hard little nuggets like salt
to keep the lies at bay

watching like an alchemist
for honesty to grow
      and burn words into gold

but
truths and lies are bed mates
squeezing in on one another
until I am just left
with salt in my eyes
      blind

phases

histories

there are stories
you would hate to reveal
that you wrote on me
in bruises

making up

this smear of red lipstick
on toilet paper
looks like blood

looks like
throwing away pieces of myself

looks like
dying for your approval

bitter dregs

I remember
drinking espresso
with you

smooth,
and a little bitter

and I didn't know
then
how well it would capture
our friendship

salt cave

you used the word "salty"
            your disenchanted self
I think of you when I hear the word

            you

and the taste of tears

the spell

in dreams I follow you
through haunted rooms
never sure
why I am here

you keep handing
me something
but when I look
it's disappeared

letters to the dead

I am still trying
to write you back to life
I try to push the poems
through the veil
to you

You never write back.

I am still writing.
You are still gone.

scrub

I am still trying
to wash off
the bruises
you left
on me

loyalty

how many nights
of waking
how many hours
measured in heartbeats
        and breaths
as the nightmares run amok
in me
have you battled at my side
always
always
      pulling me back
              toward the light

hold

holding again

as a child
I could never imagine
such a thing as
   hold

or how much of my life
would be spent in that state
hovering
somewhere between
  desiring
and
  receiving
attention

valentine's day

this day of lovers
is cold
so cold
I can't feel my knees
my lips are tingling

far from here
every long lost lover
of mine
will crawl into the warmth
of another's arms
and that
is just what I would want
is just what I want

old friends

Grief still visits
we are old friends by now
we pick the scabs off together
we watch the memories flow
we ask all the same questions
       that never had answers
       and never will
Grief pats my back as I cry
we agree
       as always
that the love was worth this price

valentine

because there was a time
when I crumpled like old tissue
and you gently
     with soft smiles and songs
and a pull out couch to cushion my spine
reminded my backbone
how to be upright
how to stack vertebrae
against the gravity of loss
you never explained the magic
just worked it
building bridges
     and backbones
with smiles and songs

cold

I will bring you
all of my dead flowers
if you will breathe me
a promise of spring

the void

the only thing
that fills the void
is pulling things
out of it

.

Spring

the warmth, the growth, the healing

phases

spring

new beginnings

this spring is a changeable
        gritty thing
a stained newspaper world
all streaks of grey and white
a dusting of silt
        mud clinging

some stains
        cannot be washed away
some changes
        are forever

85

phases

birth of man

you grow from our bodies
expansive
proud as mountains
       pushing out
       pushing down
           rising with screams
                and blood
          you grow from our bodies

spring

perseverance

you can pluck my petals
but your fingers could never dig deep enough
to touch my roots

I bloom again

healing magic

whether from string
>> or fabric
>> or ink and soul junk

the making
is the only thing
that binds me back together

spring

growth

I have been growing
back to myself
like a flower
leaning toward the sun

no matter how great the distance
I will not let
the darkness
steal my blooming
any longer

relearning

I never noticed the distance
the worlds that stood between
when we walked side by side.
Cleanly divided like borders on a map
and we just talked around them
like we didn't even know they were there —
invisible lines drawing boundaries
on how long to look, when to laugh,
how to touch, when to glance.
The boundaries pulling at us
like a puppeteer at strings,
playing at platonic.

The day the walls came down
my balance fell askew
the paths I walked no longer familiar,
I nearly crashed into you.
Your touch was a surprise,
it broke the rules we had known.
In shock I looked too long,
I blurted things, I laughed too much.
I forgot myself, I forgot the rules
and in forgetting learned something new.

promise

1) Something that, like a heart, can be broken
2) Something that, like a life, can be made

phases

love languages

love
>was learning to read
>your vulnerability
>like a foreign language

in your mind

Your bright eyes
do not see what is here —
they look past
to a place I'll never see.

What do your blue eyes hide?
A world where
your ruptured sentences
are understood;
where language is optional,
where smell, sight, taste, touch
        and sound
are interchangeable?

Is the grass greener there?
Is the sky a brighter blue?
Does the sunshine have a sound;
the wind a taste?

The questions I would love to ask
but that you'd never hear —
lost in a place I can never go,
somewhere behind your bright eyes.

tell me

tell me
about the flowers that bloom
in your mind
when the earth
sits between you
and the sun

tell me
about the gardens you grow
in the soft darkness
behind your eyelids

tell me
about the forests that stand
tall and brave as souls
in the realms
between your ears

tell me
about night magic
and the songs sung
to the distant stars
by the stardust in your bones

tell me
about beauty

spring

tell me
about dreams

tell me
about hope

tell me

travel

the bus hisses,
a rolling rectangular prism
of glass and steel,
hungry for black miles

people, tired as the morning,
reluctant bags in tow,
file into its vertical jaw
in silence

yielding the power
to separate or unite
> family
> friends
> lovers

the bus waits, indifferent as the sun.

it groans, jerks from the stationary.
a gleaming Fate,
it speeds toward everything
that cannot be seen
or measured by highway signs.

headless white arrows
lead down black paths

silent omens

spring

pointing to the horizon and away;
joining, breaking—
futures and pasts.

infrastructure

these roads map my stories
carry them back to me
in yellowed lines and scribbled cracks
leading me to the places I know
where my memories are home

bloom

there is no point
in uprooting yourself
to prove to others
that you can bloom

bruises

bruises
      bloom
            spread
        recede

coloured waves painting
               my skin
harbingers of recovery
       testimonies to damage
          inflicted in places
I will never see

scars

i do not hate
        the scars
they hold me together
        binding flesh
and experience
        in gnarled lines

spring snows

the morning snow
is a dusting of icing sugar
sweet and white
in the dawn
melting away
    with the first licks
        of sunshine

spring

sunshine

holding onto hope
sometimes feels like
		grasping sunlight
no matter how warm
it seeps through my fingers
but
I will
		always
still reach for the sun
with outstretched hands

spring

It was you.
>A grey spring
>with promise of blue skies hovering
>it was you--
>the song in my head
>and the flutter of my heart.

So many years.
The years are good.

It isn't you.
>A new grey spring
>new blue skies hovering
>it isn't you--
>my own song to sing,
>my own fluttering heart.

It is okay to learn to dance again
even if it isn't with you.
It is okay
>for spring to come again.

love has feathers

the mourning dove
in our yard
has found a mate

they are soft
rosygreybrown
with gentle coos
they tuck their faces
against each other's
throats

when separate
they wail
tremulous sobs
echoing between them--
even the span of our yard
a heavy distance
on their frail hearts

anyone
who does not believe
that love has feathers
has never witnessed
mourning doves in love
fluttering like a heart
crying for togetherness

spring defiance

I would rather

        m

          e

           l

            t

with the spring

than

       b l o o m

on demand

hope

the colour of hope
will always be green
        unfurling in spring
            despite winter's last gasps
        pushing up through sidewalk cracks
        blooming deep and soft on forest floors
wherever there is green
there is something
that has set down roots
        in determination
        in defiance
        in persistence

        in hope

coming home

the sky as I leave my
                real job
is periwinkle
                bluegreypurple
the fresh fallen snow glares
at the slowly expanding daylight

this is how spring arrives
not in blooms
but seeping shades of blue and grey

perhaps this is how I return to myself
not in flares
but the slow seep
                of expanding light

To You

if i could
i would take your hand
i would tell you
          that kindness
is your superpower

but

being kind
does not involve
          throwing yourself
on the swords of others
just because
they want blood
          and you can bleed

phases

the poems

Acknowledgements

This project would not have been possible without the overwhelming, support, advice, feedback and, of course, reading of many people.
Thank you, from my mind, heart and pen to:

Daniel Leblanc
Sarah Cotnam
Rachel Spence of Whirky Creative
Jessica Tunney
Jill Maw
Jodie Duxbury
Dayna Duxbury
Jocelyn Gard of Joceeloo Designs
Adele Scott
Julie Bratzel
Ben Hrynyk

Special thanks to Caitlin Conlon, for your inspiring piece, *Linguistics*, as well as all of the other beautiful words you give the world, and the kind advice and feedback you offered me while I was creating this book. Caitlin Conlon can be found on Instagram @cgcpoems.

h.duxbury

lives with her partner in Ontario, Canada, where she was born and raised. When she is not writing, she enjoys hiking, camping, crafting, and spoiling her cat rotten.
This is her debut collection of poetry.

More poems by h.duxbury can be found on Instagram @hduxburypoetry

A note on type:

Typeface used for body is Book Antiqua, size 11.

Typeface used for titles and subtitles is Homemade Apple, designed by Font Diner. Licensing information available at
https://www.fontsquirrel.com/license/homemade-apple

Manufactured by Amazon.ca
Bolton, ON

34228927R00076